Getting a Haircut

Isabel Anderson

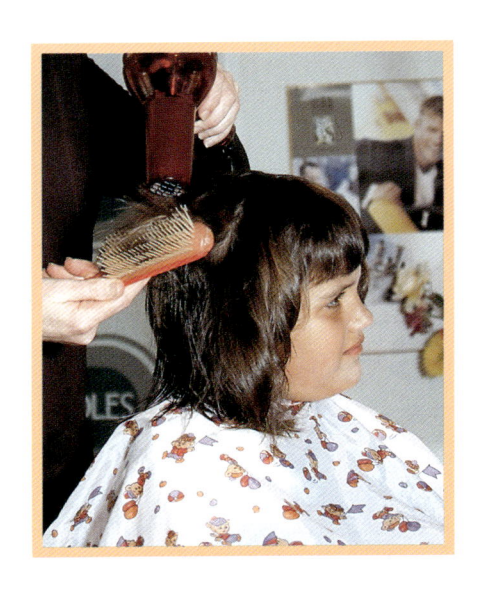

I am getting a haircut today.
Dad says my hair is too long.

Dad called the beauty shop.
The hairdresser knows I am coming.

The hairdresser smiles at me.
She knows my name.

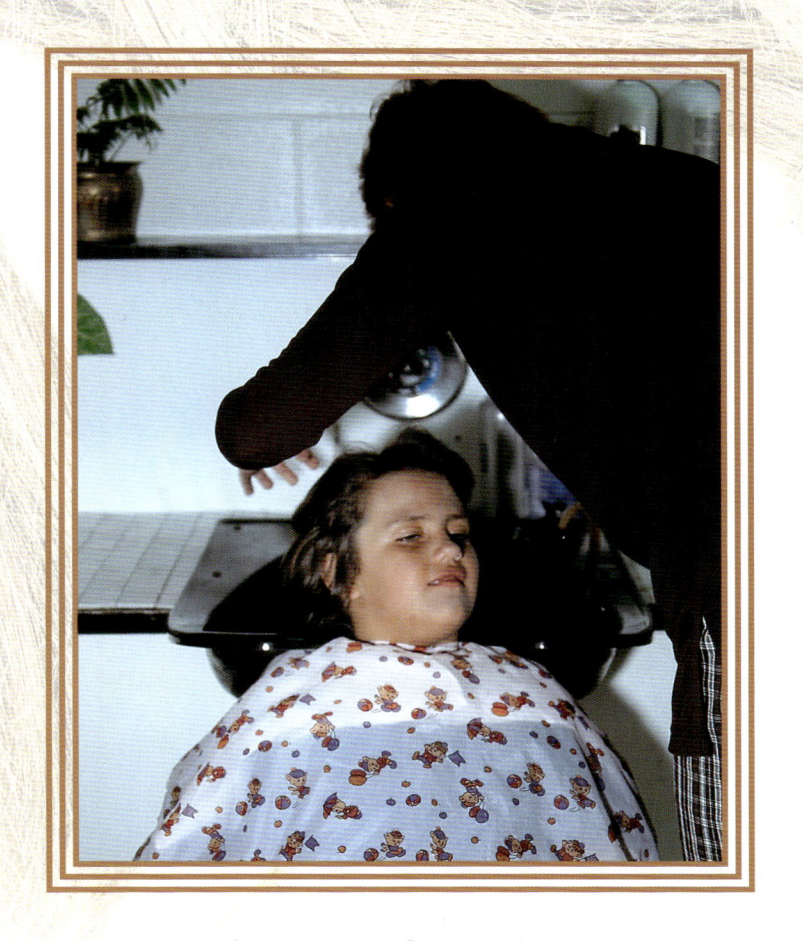

I sit in front of a sink
and lean all the way back.
I wear a plastic gown
so my clothes don't get wet.

The hairdresser puts shampoo
in my hair.
It smells good.
She washes my hair until it is clean.

I sit in a special chair.
I can see myself in the mirror.

The hairdresser cuts my bangs.
Then she cuts my hair all around.

I can see Dad watching
in the mirror.

The hairdresser dries my hair
with a blow-dryer.
It feels hot.
She brushes my hair
at the same time.

The hairdresser shows me
what my haircut looks like
from the back!
I like my new haircut.

Dad likes my haircut, too.
He pays the hairdresser.
I look at Dad's hair.
I think it is too long.
Dad needs a haircut, too.